Coping with Tourette Syndrome

A Workbook for Kids with Tic Disorders

SANDRA BUFFOLANO, MA

Instant Help Books
A Division of New Harbinger Publications, Inc.

Distributed in Canada by Raincoast Books

Copyright © 2008 by Sandra Buffolano
                Instant Help Books
                A Division of New Harbinger Publications, Inc.
                5674 Shattuck Avenue
                Oakland, CA 94609
                www.newharbinger.com

Cover design by Amy Shoup
Illustrated by Julie Olson

Library of Congress Cataloging-in-Publication Data on file with publisher

10   09   08

10   9   8   7   6   5   4   3   2   1

First printing

Dedicated to my daughter, Lauren,
whose courage and love inspires me to try
to make life easier for others with Tourette syndrome

Contents

Introduction for Mental Health Professionals

Children with Tourette syndrome face a unique set of issues that are distinctive to the disorder and require innovative management. While tics and tic disorders are the signs by which Tourette disorder is diagnosed, it is the related conditions that comprise the "syndrome" and make management difficult. These comorbid disorders—obsessive-compulsive disorder, attention-deficit/hyperactivity disorder, learning problems, and anxiety—are addressed in the activities in *Managing Tourette Syndrome*. This workbook is also helpful for dealing with PANDAS, or pediatric autoimmune neuropsychiatric disorders associated with streptococcal infection.

Although the term "counselor" has been used throughout the activities for simplicity, this book is designed for use by psychologists, therapists, and school psychologists. Several activities focus on skills that help children succeed in school. It is also written from the perspective that parents are important partners. Some activities ask children to seek their parents' input, and parents may want to share newly gained knowledge with mental health professionals or school personnel.

While some children find it possible to suppress their tics for short periods, doing so often results in a period of greater intensity and frequency of symptoms. For this reason, many activities present alternative solutions.

It is recommended that the activities be completed in the order given, as some build on previously acquired knowledge. For example, the characteristic waxing and waning of TS symptoms has been analogized to the phases of the moon. Grasping the analogy, which is presented early on, is important to understanding later activities. Some activities are situational and can be completed out of order or as the situation, such as visiting relatives or going shopping, arises. Many activities address concerns that are common to all children, although these concerns often have a stronger impact on children with TS.

A Note to Parents

Tourette syndrome is a chronic neurological condition characterized by multiple motor and vocal tics that persist for more than a year. Naturally, the symptoms of Tourette cause a great deal of stress in children, but the problem is often exacerbated by self-esteem issues, difficulty with peers, and a variety of behavioral problems, including hyperactivity, distractibility, aggressiveness, and sleep disorders.

But even though Tourette syndrome is a chronic condition, children can learn new skills to cope with their symptoms, and they can live happy and fulfilling lives. Written by Sandra Buffolano, a psychologist with over eighteen years experience in working with children who have Tourette syndrome, this workbook goes a long way to teaching children practical skills. By going through the activities in the book, children will not only learn for themselves about their problem, but will be able to explain it to others. They will learn to be more self-confident, to plan ahead in order to make their symptoms easier to handle, and to ask for help when they need it.

Children learn emotional and behavioral skills just like they learn academic or athletic skills, through practice and encouragement. Your child will likely need your guidance in going through this workbook, and he or she will certainly need your encouragement.

As you help your child, you will probably find out that it is difficult for him to talk about certain issues. Never force your child to talk if he doesn't want to. The best way to get children to open up is to be a good role model. Talk about your thoughts, feelings, and experiences as they relate to each activity, stressing the positive ways that you cope with problems. Even if your child doesn't say a thing back, your words will have an impact on his behavior.

There is no wrong way to use this workbook to help your child as long as you remain patient and respectful of your child's feelings. If your child is being seen by a counselor, make sure you share this workbook with the therapist. She may have some additional ideas on how best to use the activities.

Tourette syndrome can be very difficult for children as well as their families. Your patience and understanding will make all the difference.

Sincerely,

Lawrence E. Shapiro, PhD

A Special Message to Parents

I, too, am the parent of a wonderful child who faces Tourette syndrome every day. After fourteen years of being Lauren's mom and eighteen years of working with other families, I have learned a few things to pass on to you.

This adventure began when your child was born. Your life may not have gone as you planned. It probably took twists and turns; it may have stalled at times. Most likely, your child had an early diagnosis that was incorrect or incomplete. Maybe there were many different diagnoses that all proved correct and were all part of Tourette syndrome.

Your money, insurance, time, and patience have probably all been stretched thin. But with those stretches, you have learned more about yourself and your child. With this book, your child will learn more about himself or herself and TS.

I wish for you a journey full of good people, knowledgeable doctors and psychologists, understanding teachers who use their talents to foster your child's self-esteem, and lots of fun with your child. If you do not find these, keep looking. Change doctors, conference with teachers, provide information to your psychologists, choose afterschool care carefully, and inform your relatives.

We are our children's advocates until they can be their own. They will follow where we lead and be stronger and happier because of our efforts.

Sincerely,

Sandra

A Message to Young Readers

Dear Kids,

You already have plenty of experience living with Tourette syndrome, so do you really need homework to practice? Well, the activities in this book are different from the homework you are used to. This workbook is designed to help you understand TS and cope with the things that bug you about having it. Here are some of the great things that can start to happen when you learn more about yourself:

- You will worry less about your problems.
- You will understand why your TS changes.
- You will be able to explain TS to others.
- You will be able to ask for help when you need it.
- You will become more confident.

Your counselor can help you with the activities in this workbook. Counselors have the very special job of helping children. They know that it is sometimes hard to handle TS, and they know that there are other adults who can help as well. As you complete the activities, your parents will also learn a lot about you and your TS. When you and the adults in your life work together on a project like this, here are some more great things that can happen:

- You will learn how to work as a team to solve problems.
- You will see all the progress you have made.
- You will learn to plan ahead to make your TS easier to handle.
- You will enjoy working together, when it is fun and even when it is hard.

There are also local chapters of the Tourette Syndrome Association, where you can find out about other people with TS. Their Web address is **http://tsa-usa.org**, and they even have a newsletter just for kids!

Sincerely,
Sandra

What Is Tourette Syndrome?

Brandon was ten years old. He was good at playing the guitar, and he loved to do card tricks. Even when he didn't mean to, Brandon often blinked and cleared his throat. Sometimes he clicked his tongue and shook his head. He had started to make these unusual movements and sounds just before he turned nine.

When Brandon's mom took him for a checkup, the doctor asked them both many questions. Here is what they told the doctor:

- Brandon made certain noises again and again, but he didn't know why.
- He repeated certain movements many times, and again, he didn't know why.
- Sometimes his noises and movements happened more often and sometimes less often.
- They had been happening since before his last birthday.

Their answers helped the doctor decide that Brandon had Tourette syndrome. The doctor explained that Brandon's noises and movements were called tics and they were part of his Tourette syndrome. He told Brandon that the tics were not his fault and that TS was only part of who he was. He was still the boy who liked to play the guitar and was good at card tricks. He was still Brandon.

What Is Tourette Syndrome?

Directions

Take some time to think about how having TS affects you, and then write the answers to the questions below. If you want to, ask your parents to help you.

What bothers you about having TS? _____

_____

_____

What would you like to know about your TS? _____

_____

_____

Whom can you talk to about it? _____

_____

_____

What bothers your parents about TS? _____

_____

_____

What would they like to know about your TS? _____

_____

_____

What Is Tourette Syndrome?

Having Tourette syndrome is only part of who you are. Now let's talk about you and everything but Tourette syndrome. Fill in the blanks below:

My name is _____.

I am _____ years old and I am in the _____ grade.

I live with _____.

I have _____ brothers and _____ sisters.

I like to play _____.

I am good at _____.

My friends are _____.

On the weekends I like to _____.

The name of my school is _____.

My favorite class is _____.

I eat lunch with _____.

In the box below, draw a picture of you doing something you really enjoy.

When Ethan's doctor first explained about tics, Ethan and his father had different reactions. Ethan thought the word was weird, so he laughed. His father thought Ethan's doctor was talking about insects. The doctor drew a funny cartoon of a tic and a tick to help them understand.

He explained that there are two kinds of tics: vocal tics and motor tics. Vocal tics are sounds, like sniffing or coughing. Repeating words or lines from a movie are also vocal tics. Motor tics involve movement, like blinking or jerking.

Ethan thought about his own tics, and he realized that they were different at different times. When he played video games or practiced playing the piano, his tics would stop for a while. When he was thinking hard, they didn't seem to bother him either. His tics were more of a problem at school, because he had to be there all day and couldn't take a break from class. He would try to stop shaking his head and keep his noises inside. Sometimes it worked for a while, and sometimes it didn't work at all. Trying to keep quiet often made it harder for him to do his schoolwork. When he was excited or upset, it was really hard. Sometimes just thinking about his noises made them worse!

When Ethan was with his parents or hanging out with good friends, he often made more sounds and movements, but his parents and friends didn't mind. They knew that he couldn't help it and that it felt better for him to do those things than to try not to.

Ethan decided to make a list of things he had learned about tics. Here is what he wrote:

1. Some kids have tics that are very different from mine.

2. The most important thing I have learned about tics is that they can change.

3. Sometimes tics get better and sometimes they get worse. Sometimes they even go away for a while.

4. When kids get older, their tics may get better.

5. Sometimes a new tic can just pop up.

6. You can't hold in tics for long amounts of time.

7. If you try to hold in tics for too long, they'll burst out later.

8. My family and friends have gotten used to my tics and often don't notice them after a while.

Directions

Tics are sounds or movements that you do over and over and have a hard time stopping. Use a highlighter to mark tics that you have had.

Sounds (Vocal Tics)	**Movements (Motor Tics)**
Clearing your throat	Blinking
Humming	Moving your eyebrows or nose
Sniffing	Making faces
Smacking your lips	Moving your shoulders
Kissing	Putting your arm out
Clicking your tongue	Bending over
Grunting	Hopping
Whispering	Jumping
Hawking	Shaking, jerking, or rolling your head
Spitting	Pulling at your clothes
Blowing raspberries	Smelling
Coughing repeatedly	Tensing your muscles
Repeating words	Kicking
Whistling	Biting
Cursing	Cracking your knuckles or joints
Barking	Touching other people
Imitating others	Touching things
Other _____	Other _____

Did some of your tics start and then stop?   Yes   No

If you answered yes, tell which ones. _____

Did some go away and come back?   Yes   No

If you answered yes, tell which ones. _____

Did you ever get new tics when you felt stressed?   Yes   No

If you answered yes, tell which ones. _____

Are any of your tics embarrassing?   Yes   No

If you answered yes, tell which ones. _____

Share the list of your tics with your parents, and ask if they knew about all of them. Then ask if they have noticed any tics you didn't realize you had.

If there is anything else you would like to share about your tics, write it here.

_____

_____

_____

_____

Activity 3

The Phases of Tourette Syndrome

In science class, Cody had learned about how the moon looked bigger and smaller in different phases. To help him think about how Tourette syndrome affected him, his counselor suggested that he compare it to the phases of the moon. Here is what Cody came up with:

When my TS is like a crescent moon, I have fewer tics and I feel happy most of the time.

When my TS is like a half moon, I feel frustrated. It is hard for me to finish my schoolwork and my chores at home.

When my TS is like a three-quarter moon, it is hard for me to handle. I worry more, and I need more help from my parents and teachers.

When my TS is like a full moon, I feel like saying, "Forget it!" I get angry, so I talk with my counselor more often. I need help from grown-ups to explain to other kids what is happening.

Directions

Think about how your TS changes and fill in the chart below.

Moon Phase	What My TS Is Like	How I Feel
Crescent		
Half		
Three Quarter		
Full		

What is today like for you? _____

_____

_____

What phase of the moon is it like? _____

What was last week like? _____

_____

_____

How was it different from today? How was it similar? _____

_____

_____

Think about a time when you had a lot of fun and found school easier. Draw the phase of the moon that time was like.

```

```

Think about a time that was really hard for you. Draw the phase of the moon that time was like.

```

```

Planning Ahead for Your TS Phases

Jordan was having a rough week. His TS was in more than a half-moon phase, but not yet a full moon. His thoughts were getting stuck on playing video games, and he begged his parents to buy him new ones. He couldn't wait for school to be over so he could go home and play. He even turned down a friend's invitation to ride bikes after school so that he could play more video games; he wanted to beat his last score. Jordan's mother had to set a timer for him or he would have played video games all night long.

His tics were worse, too. His handwriting was poor, and he had to take more breaks from his work. He left things at home that he needed for school, and he forgot things at school that he needed at home. He had to study longer to pass his tests, too. Jordan knew it was not his fault, but he still felt bad about his schoolwork.

When Jordan met with his counselor, they talked about the fact that he had harder and easier times with his TS; sometimes it was like a full moon and sometimes like a crescent moon. She explained that Jordan could learn to recognize the signs that a full-moon phase was coming: for example, when he started to be more forgetful or when it became harder for him to write neatly. They agreed on a plan to help Jordan. Knowing that a full-moon phase would be coming, he would get ahead on his schoolwork when he was in a crescent-moon phase. When writing neatly became a problem, he would type his assignments. At home, he worked out a plan with his parents. He would do more chores so that he could earn money for a new video game.

Activity 4   Planning Ahead for Your TS Phases

Directions

For each phase of your TS, describe a behavior that happens and tell what you can do to try to make life easier. For example, you may get along better with other kids in your crescent-moon phase, so that is a good time to have a friend over. In your full-moon phase, it may be very hard for you to concentrate, so you can help yourself by breaking projects into smaller pieces.

Moon Phase	Behavior	What I Can Do
Crescent		
Half		
Three Quarter		
Full		

Plan ahead for the next five days based on what phase your TS is in now. List an activity that you know is coming up on each day, and then write what you will try to help make that day easier.

Day 1 activity _____

To help make that day easier, I will _____

_____

Day 2 activity _____

To help make that day easier, I will _____

_____

Day 3 activity _____

To help make that day easier, I will _____

_____

Day 4 activity _____

To help make that day easier, I will _____

_____

Day 5 activity _____

To help make that day easier, I will _____

_____

Although Tyler and Emma each worried about different things, they both worried a lot. Their school counselor, Ms. Martinez, invited them to join a group she had started to help kids who were anxious. She explained that anxiety was just another word for worrying and that everyone worried sometimes. But some kids worried so much that it ruined things they wanted to do, and some kids were so anxious that they didn't even try to do things.

Ms. Martinez taught them to think about their worries using a "worry thermometer" with a scale from 1 to 10. Number 1 on the scale stood for a very calm feeling, like taking a nap in a warm place. Number 10 on the scale stood for really big fears, like feeling that you were about to die. When she asked Tyler how he would rate thunder, he placed it at 2 and said he likes to watch the lightning. Emma said that when she hears thunder she hides her eyes and can't wait for it to stop. She placed it at 7 on the scale. Ms. Martinez said that when kids rated their worries, adults could better understand how to help them.

Directions

How much do you worry about each of the items below? Draw a line from each item to the number on the thermometer that shows how much you worry about it.

Car trips

Company coming

Eating lunch in the cafeteria

Eating dinner at home

Getting a haircut

Going to the doctor

Homework

Math class

Nightmares

Reading a book

Recess

Spelling tests

Thunder

Visiting the school nurse

Weekends

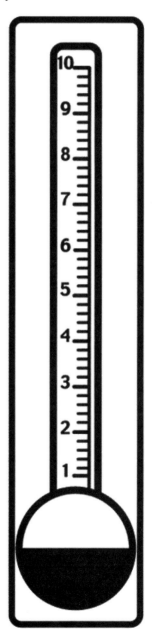

Now think of other events in your life, and use this thermometer to rate them. Try to include each of these:

- Things you do every day, like brushing your teeth
- Things you do a few times a year, like going to the dentist
- Things you may have done only a few times, like going to a wedding

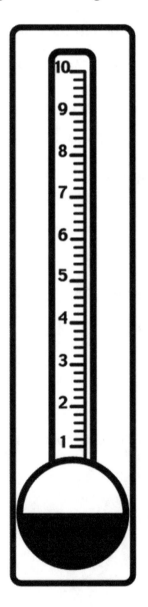

_____

_____

_____

_____

_____

_____

_____

_____

_____

_____

_____

_____

_____

TS and OCD

Robert had Tourette syndrome and he also had obsessive-compulsive disorder (OCD). His OCD made him think about certain things, like video games and baseball, over and over. Sometimes he could think about baseball for just a few minutes and then stop, but he thought about video games so much that he would forget to do his chores. At school, he got in trouble for drawing pictures about his video games. It was an obsession that he couldn't stop thinking about.

When Robert's OCD made him think about baseball, he sometimes made a swinging motion with his arms, as if he were at bat. Then he felt like he had to do it two more times to make three strikes. That type of behavior, which Robert couldn't always stop, was called a compulsion. Collecting baseball cards was also an obsession for him. He wanted to buy more and more. His parents told him that he couldn't possibly collect them all, but Robert kept trying. He had temper tantrums when he wanted his parents to give him money to buy more cards.

Robert found it hard when his OCD got him in trouble with his teachers or parents. He tried to tell himself, "Don't do that!" That didn't always work, so his counselor helped him come up with a plan. One part of the plan was for Robert's parents to put his video games in a locked closet that they would unlock only when Robert could use the games. Another part of Robert's plan was to let Robert act on some of his smaller obsessions so that they didn't build up in his head. For example, he was allowed to touch things three times.

Directions

Work with your parent to complete this activity. In the space below, list any obsessive thoughts or compulsive behaviors you may have.

Obsessions	**Compulsions**
_____	_____
_____	_____
_____	_____
_____	_____
_____	_____
_____	_____
_____	_____

Have your parent help you monitor these for a week. If you become aware of any more obsessions or compulsions, add them to this list.

Major OCD thoughts or behaviors are those that stop you from doing what you are supposed to do for long periods of time. They may cause you to get into trouble with adults. Some can even cause you to be hurt, for example, biting your nails until they bleed. You may also have minor OCD thoughts or behaviors that you did not even list. Minor OCD thoughts and behaviors, such as constantly licking your lips, might even be called bad habits by other people.

List any of your OCD thoughts or behaviors that are major here: _____

_____

_____

If you have any OCD thoughts or behaviors that are minor, list them here: _____

_____

_____

Chelsea had tics, and she also had attention-deficit/hyperactivity disorder, or ADHD. Her ADHD made it hard for her to pay attention, so she had to ask her teacher to repeat instructions. Chelsea was disorganized, too. Her schoolwork was often messy. Even when she remembered to do her homework, she sometimes forgot to bring it to school the next day.

It was also difficult for Chelsea to sit still in class. When she was supposed to be quiet, she often called out or jumped out of her seat. At recess, the other kids left her out of their games because she didn't want to wait her turn.

Directions

Below each picture, write what these kids could do to help them be more organized or pay attention.

_____

_____

_____

_____

_____

_____

_____

_____

_____

_____

_____

_____

Even kids who don't have ADHD sometimes have trouble paying attention or being organized or staying still. Tell about a time when you had a problem like that.

_____

_____

_____

_____

What could you have done differently? _____

_____

_____

_____

List three ideas that will help you be more organized.

1. _____

_____

2. _____

_____

3. _____

_____

Explaining TS to Others

Danielle's most frequent vocal tics were grunting and whistling. Sometimes these tics were loud enough for others to hear in class. She felt embarrassed and wanted her teachers and others at school to understand that she couldn't stop the noises.

Danielle and her parents met with her teacher and the school nurse to talk about TS and tics. Together, they came up with a plan to help Danielle explain her TS to others and feel more comfortable in school. They decided that Danielle could say this:

> I have Tourette syndrome. Have you heard me grunt and whistle? That's part of my TS. There are other things my body and brain make me do, too. Sometimes I can stop for a little while, but then I can't concentrate on anything else. Trying to stop takes a lot of energy, and it is very hard. I'm sorry if I'm bothering you. TS is something I would like to control, but I can't. I would if I could.

After that meeting, when Danielle had a loud tic, her teacher ignored the noise. The other kids in Danielle's class learned to ignore it, too. They understood that all people are different and Danielle's tics were part of who she was.

This plan seemed to work well for everyone, and Danielle felt better at school.

Directions

Plan a script to explain your TS. You can fill in the blanks below or write your own script on a separate piece of paper.

I have Tourette syndrome. Have you noticed that I _____? That's part of my TS. There are other things my body and brain make me do, too. Sometimes I can stop for a little while, but then I can't concentrate on anything else. Trying to stop takes a lot of energy, and it is very hard. I'm sorry if I'm bothering you. TS is something I would like to control, but I can't. I would if I could.

When do you think this script would work for you? _____

_____

_____

Practice the script with your parent, counselor, or another adult until you feel comfortable saying the words without looking at them. Next, choose a relative that you talk to a lot. Ask if you can practice your script together, in person or over the phone. When you feel good about that practice, share it with another relative or friend.

Use the log on the next page to keep a record of your practice.

Date	Person I Practiced With	How My Practice Went

Activity 9

Answering Questions Quickly

Conner wanted to be more comfortable about his TS around strangers. He found it helpful to have a friend or relative nearby when his TS was noticeable. On weekends, he liked to go to the video store with his uncle. They would pick out movies for Saturday nights and try out new video games so they could decide which to buy. When they played games, Conner's tics were less noticeable, but when they looked for videos, he often did a lot of clicking and head shaking. If no one paid attention to his tics, Connor and his uncle would just continue what they were doing. But sometimes, people stared at him or asked questions. Then Connor used a short script that he had practiced:

I have Tourette syndrome. I'm sorry, but I just can't stop. I would if I could.

Directions

Tourette syndrome is often noticeable, and people may ask you about it. If you have thought in advance about what you will say, you may feel more comfortable answering their questions. Ask your parent or another adult to help you plan what you could say if any of these people ask about your TS. Use the space below to write your answers.

Someone you've just met _____

_____

_____

A substitute teacher _____

_____

_____

A friend you've known for a while _____

_____

_____

The person who cuts your hair _____

_____

_____

A relative you don't see often _____

_____

_____

Sometimes you may be in situations where you have only a short time to explain Tourette syndrome. You can simply say, "I have Tourette syndrome. I'm sorry, but I just can't stop. I would if I could."

When do you think this short script would work for you? _____

_____

_____

_____

_____

Brad Cohen is an elementary school teacher and coauthor of *Front of the Class: How Tourette Syndrome Made Me the Teacher I Never Had*, a book about having Tourette syndrome. He has very noticeable tics that often make people look at him. His tics are loud and sudden, so he has had to get used to people staring at him every day. Here is an interview with Brad:

Brad, would you describe your Tourette syndrome as mild, moderate, or severe?

My TS is a severe case because my vocal tics are so apparent.

What are your most noticeable tics?

I make loud barking sounds. Some people call them a "whop" sound, while others say it is a "dra" or "bah" sound. Either way, they are loud enough to put a lot of attention on me. I also have facial tics that cause me to make funny faces or violent twitches with my neck.

When do you find that people stare at you?

Always! People are always staring at me. Over time I have gotten used to it. It is obviously worse when the people are not familiar with TS. But even once they do know I have TS, they are still looking.

What do you do when that happens?

At first, nothing. I just let it happen. I understand that my noises and tics are different. At first, people will look because they just don't know what's going on. Then those that do realize I have TS, they stop staring a little bit. Those who are not familiar with TS will either continue staring or they will keep looking back every few minutes.

Sometimes when those people just keep staring and don't stop, I'll just stare back. That usually causes them to stop. If I have an opportunity to educate them, I will. But most of the time, I'm only around the stranger for a short period of time and I don't get a chance to explain.

What is your best advice for kids who have very noticeable tics that make people stare at them?

Don't let the stares bother you. Get used to it. After a while, you will actually get used to the stares. When I go out in public, my friends and family get more upset by the stares than I do. I guess since I have lived with TS for so long, I'm used to it. I have tried to live my life just like anyone else, and I don't allow the stares from other people to get in the way of me living my life to the fullest!

Directions

Think about a time when you were stared at. Where were you? _____

_____

_____

What happened? _____

_____

_____

What did you do? _____

_____

_____

Do you think that was a good way to handle it? If not, what else could you have done?

_____

_____

_____

_____

Circle the places where you would feel okay handling stares:

at home	on the school bus	in a public restroom
in homeroom	in music class	getting your picture taken at school
in the lunchroom	at a family party	walking home
in a restaurant	at camp	at a scout meeting
at a sleepover	in a car	at a ball game
at a grocery store	during recess	at your place of worship

other _____

Some kids feel more comfortable in familiar situations, like when they are at school or when their parents are around. Is there a pattern to when you feel okay?

_____

_____

When would you ignore the stares? _____

_____

_____

When would you try to explain? _____

_____

_____

What would you do if someone teased you? _____

_____

_____

One day, Jackson's health teacher brought a wheelchair to class. The kids in the class took turns sitting in the wheelchair. They had a chance to feel what not being able to walk might be like. Another day, they each kept their eyes closed for an entire class period to see what being blind was like.

Jackson had practiced his TS script with his parents and shared it with other people, but he wished that his classmates, his friends, and his family could experience what having TS was like. He knew that if other people understood about his TS, he would feel more relaxed. He would be able to express his tics without worrying about what others thought. He met with his school psychologist to come up with an idea. Together, they created "The Tourette Syndrome Game." That night, Jackson played the game with his mom. She said it really helped her understand.

Directions

You can play The Tourette Syndrome Game with a parent, a relative, a friend, a teacher, or anyone who has a few minutes to spare. All you need is a timer, or you can use a clock or a watch. Before you play, fill in the blanks below:

One of my vocal tics is _____.

One of my motor tics is _____.

My favorite number under ten is _____.

Then read the following out loud, inserting your answers:

The Tourette Syndrome Game can help you understand what having TS is like. You must follow the rules and then tell me how you feel at the end. When I say "Go," you will start singing "Happy Birthday." You will keep singing for two minutes. Each time you sing the word "happy," you will do my phonic tic, which is _____. Each time you sing the word "birthday," you will do my motor tic, which is _____. Each time you sing the word "you," you will clap your hands as many times as my favorite number, which is _____.

Read the directions twice and then start timing. If other players ask you to read the rules again, you can, but don't stop timing. You can't help them, but you can correct them. At the end of two minutes, say "Stop."

Then ask the other players the following questions.

1. How did you feel before you started playing this game?
2. How did you feel in the middle of the game?
3. How did you feel at the end of this game?
4. Were you able to sing "Happy Birthday" as many times as you expected?
5. Was it harder than you thought it would be?
6. Is there anything else you want to share with me?

Who is another person you would like to play this game with? _____

Masking Tics

Have you ever tried to not sneeze or to not hiccup? Sometimes you can actually make sneezes or hiccups less noticeable, but a lot of times you can't. Have you ever thought about your tics in the same way? There are times when you feel comfortable expressing your tics. There are other times when you might be more embarrassed and want to cover them up. There are also places where it is best to cover up tics and places where it doesn't matter as much.

Directions

Think about a time when one of your tics was easy to cover up.

Where were you? _____

What happened? _____

_____

Now think about a time when there was no way to cover up the same tic.

Where were you? _____

What happened? _____

_____

Do you know what the word "camouflage" means? You can use a dictionary or ask someone, and write the definition here: _____

_____

There are two ways to manage your tics. One way is to camouflage them, or try to make them less noticeable. For example, if you have a mouth movement tic, you could cover your mouth when it happens. What is another example you can think of?

_____

_____

Color this mask to help you remember that you can make your tics less noticeable. You can use the colors the army uses for camouflage or black for nighttime, or you may have your own idea.

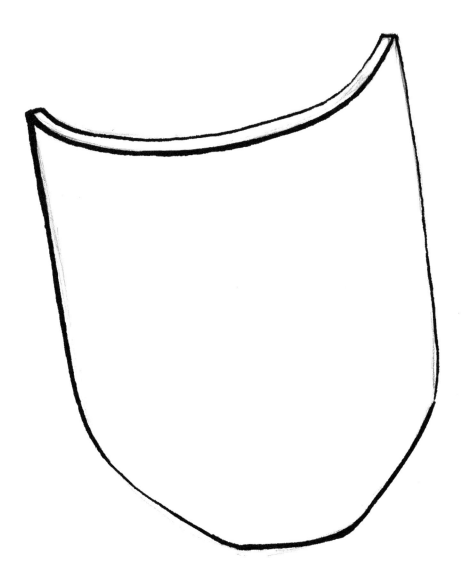

Another way to manage your tics is to distract others by making yourself big and bold. For example, your tic is constantly combing your fingers through your hair, so you spike it up with hair gel and play with it all day long. What other example can you think of?

Color this mask to help you remember that you can choose to be noticed.

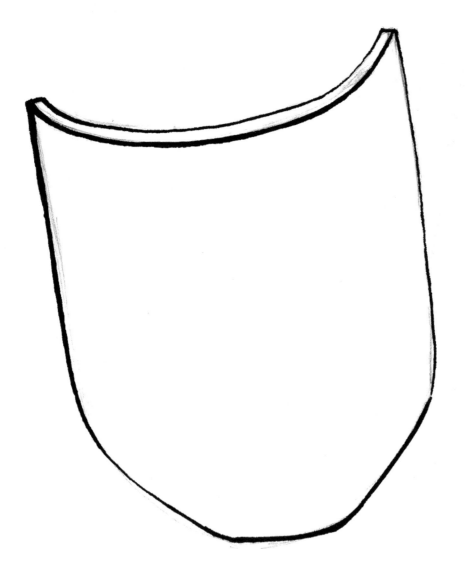

In the spaces that follow, put a C if you would use a camouflage idea. Put a B if you would use a big and bold idea.

_____ In the school library

_____ In the car with your parent

_____ Watching television at home

_____ During breakfast at your grandmother's house

_____ At a fast-food restaurant

_____ During a movie in a theater

_____ In math class

_____ In music class

_____ Meeting a new friend

_____ At the park

_____ At your own birthday party

Taylor was pretty good at covering up her tics. When she sniffed and cleared her throat often, she would pretend to have a cold and use a lot of tissues. Taylor and her counselor had worked out this idea and others to help her avoid being embarrassed.

Travis found that a lot of his tics were harder to camouflage, so he asked his counselor for ideas. Together, they decided that Travis could use humor as a way to handle his tics. When he had a lot of tongue clicking and head shaking, he could pretend to play air guitar. He could also tell jokes to help distract other kids from noticing his tics. His counselor also gave Travis this advice:

- Learn several jokes, and don't keep telling the same one.
- Some people are good at jokes, and some need to practice.
- At certain times, making people laugh can get you into trouble.
- Your teacher can help you use humor in the right way.
- Your friends can help you by laughing when you need them to.
- Knock-knock jokes can sometimes be annoying to others.

Directions

Here are some more ideas to try that can help you use humor. Put a check next to the ones you would like to try.

_____ 1. Each weekend, learn a few good jokes and tell one immediately after an embarrassing tic. This won't always work at school, especially if you are taking a test!

_____ 2. Ask your teacher to help when you make a big sound or noise that you can't control. Your teacher can say, "Bless you!" as if you had sneezed.

_____ 3. Turn a "bad" word into a different word or sound. For example, if you say "butt" as a tic, turn it into "butter."

_____ 4. Take a drama class and become a real comedian!

Write your own ideas here. _____

_____

_____

_____

_____

Ask your parent to help you decide when using humor with your tics is okay, and practice together. Remember, using humor with Tourette syndrome is like wearing a helmet when you ride a bike—it can give you some protection.

In the space below, draw a picture that helps you remember to use humor.

Dominic and Sam both had Tourette syndrome. One time Dominic was at Sam's house for a holiday party. Sam's mom had decorated the house and made a special meal. Everyone was dressed up and using their best manners. Dominic had never heard so many "pleases" and "thank-yous" before.

When Dominic and Sam were together, they didn't usually worry about their tics. But at this party, they were both doing their best to cover them up. Suddenly, Sam looked at his mom and tugged his ear. His mom nodded her head, and Sam went right to his bedroom. As soon as the door was closed, Sam let out a loud whoop. That was Sam's biggest tic.

When Sam was younger, his mom had tugged on her ear when she could tell that Sam needed to release a tic. Now that Sam was older, he tugged on his own ear to signal that he was leaving the room. His mom would nod, and Sam would go to his bedroom, which was the place he and his mom had agreed on. By using the signal, Sam didn't have to say anything or feel embarrassed, and his mom would know where he was going.

Sam had a plan at school, too. His teacher kept a special pass on her desk. When Sam needed to leave this room to release tics, he would get his teacher's permission to take the pass. Then he would go to the nurse's office.

Dominic thought that using a signal was a great idea. He decided to plan signals to use at home and school.

Directions

You may find is easier to release your tics in certain situations or with certain people. List people that you are comfortable releasing your tics in front of.

_____

_____

_____

Now, list some places where it doesn't matter if you release your tics.

_____

_____

_____

Ask your parent and your counselor to help you pick one place at home and one place at school where you can be alone to release your tics. Write these places below.

At home: _____

At school: _____

What signal could you use at home or with your parent? _____

_____

_____

What signal could you use at school? _____

_____

_____

"Bad" Words

Whenever you see symbols like the ones below in a cartoon, you know that the character is saying words that are too "bad" to print. It is called cursing, swearing, or profanity.

When a person with tics or Tourette syndrome says words that are too "bad" to print, it is called the same thing: cursing, swearing, or profanity.

But some people with Tourette syndrome can't stop saying those words, even when they want to. Those people have a tic called coprolalia. Of every hundred people who have TS, only about ten have coprolalia.

Activity 15

Directions

Think about times when you have used "bad" words, and answer the questions below.

Does coprolalia happen with your Tourette syndrome?	Yes	No
If yes, does it happen without warning?	Yes	No
Do you also use "bad" words when you are really angry?	Yes	No
Do you have any control over it?	Yes	No

If so, describe a time when you had control. _____

_____

Does your counselor know all your answers to the questions above?	Yes	No
Does your parent know all the answers to the questions above?	Yes	No
Some people with Tourette syndrome also make rude gestures. Has that ever happened with your TS?	Yes	No
Have you ever been embarrassed because of coprolalia?	Yes	No
Have you discussed this with someone at school?	Yes	No
Do you have a behavior plan that talks about what will happen if this occurs at school?	Yes	No

If you don't, whom can you talk to at school about it? _____

_____

If you do, describe it here. _____

_____

Kelsey had a good friend named Shara. They were the same age, and they knew a lot about each other. Kelsey and Shara both liked horses, and they rode together whenever they could. They wanted to go to horseback-riding camp together, so they spent a lot of time learning about camps on the Internet. Shara also knew about Kelsey's tics and helped her when Kelsey felt embarrassed. Kelsey knew that math was a hard subject for Shara, so she helped Shara study for math tests.

Kelsey also had friends who were not her age. Her neighbor Ann used to babysit for Kelsey. Now they played guitar together, and they liked to go out for ice cream. Ann and Kelsey had known each other for a long time, and even though they were different ages, they enjoyed spending time together. Kelsey had a favorite aunt that she saw on weekends. They went to the mall together, and they tried new recipes. Even though they were relatives, they acted like friends.

Directions

Put a check next to each statement you think is true about friends.

_____ A friend can be someone you know very well.

_____ A friend can be someone you met a few days ago.

_____ A friend might know your secrets.

_____ A friend doesn't share your secrets.

_____ A friend helps you when you need it.

_____ A friend respects your need to be alone.

_____ You can have more than one friend.

_____ Your friend can have other friends besides you.

Use the space below to write about what you think a good friend is, or to draw a picture that shows your idea.

Name some friends who are the same age as you. _____

_____

_____

Name some older kids who are your friends. _____

_____

_____

Name some relatives or other adults who are your friends. _____

_____

_____

Which of these friends would you like to talk with about your TS? _____

_____

_____

What would you like to say to them? _____

_____

_____

When Kayla moved to a new school, she found it hard to make friends. She had been comfortable with her old friends. They knew about her vocal tics and her movement tics, and they didn't react to them. They also understood about her obsession with ballet and were patient with her constant chatter about recitals and performances of *The Nutcracker*.

Kayla met with her counselor, and they talked about how to make new friends. They came up with these ideas:

- Watch others' body language when you walk up to them. If they turn toward you and smile or look friendly, they are interested in talking.

- Try to start a conversation with someone who is not already talking to another person. If you walk up to a group, wait for your turn to talk.

- Smile and say hello.

- Start the conversation with a topic you both know about, like school or a recent event.

- Look interested when others talk to you.

- Don't rush the friendship. Wait until you have been friends for a while before inviting people to your house.

Kayla's counselor reminded her that there were many other kids interested in making new friends. After they talked, Kayla decided that she would try these ideas.

Directions

Thinking about your old friendships can help you understand what is important to you in making new friends. In the space below, tell about friends you already have.

Your Friend's Name	What You Like to Do Together	What You Like About This Friend

List three topics you feel comfortable talking about:

1. _____

2. _____

3. _____

Write a few sentences you can use to start conversation on each of these topics. For example, if the topic is bike riding, you could say, "Hi. You have a great bike. When did you get it?"

1. _____

_____

2. _____

_____

3. _____

_____

Describe what you will do to make new friends in the next few months.

_____

_____

_____

What will you do if your TS is obvious when you are with a new friend?

_____

_____

_____

Activity 18

Different Feelings

Max and Tiffany had different feelings about different things. Max felt happy when he played baseball, but Tiffany worried that she would miss the ball. Tiffany loved roller coasters that looped, but Max hated the feeling of being upside down and was afraid that he would fall. They also had different feelings in school. When Max got a poor grade on his math test, he felt angry. When Tiffany got a poor grade in spelling, she was so sad that she felt like crying.

They each felt different about their TS, too. When Tiffany could not stop blinking her eyes in public, she felt embarrassed. When it happened with her friends, she felt comfortable. When Max made a barking noise over and over, he was sad and wished he could stop.

Directions

Use this guide to color the rainbow below:

Mad = red
Happy = orange
Worried = yellow
Embarrassed = green
Sad = blue

In the chart below, outline each face in the color that matches the feeling it shows. Then complete the chart.

Feeling	When I Feel This Way

Now tell about a time you had one of these feelings because of having TS.

_____

_____

_____

Feelings Game

When you are managing Tourette syndrome, you will have many different feelings. Learning to recognize your feeling and share them with others can help you.

Here are some examples of common feelings:

- Alexandra wanted a pair of jeans that cost more than her parents were willing to spend. Her parents told her that she had to help pay for them. When she finally saved enough money, she felt happy that she could buy the jeans.

- Vincent had saved his money for three months to buy a new video game. The first day he tried to play it, he found out that it didn't work right. He felt mad.

- Sarah had been trying to learn how to shoot foul shots, but she was having a hard time. Her cousin said he would help her. The day he came over, the basketball court in the town park was closed, so they couldn't play. She felt sad that her cousin wouldn't get to teach her after all.

- Evan and his friends went to the beach. They played in the surf all morning and had a wonderful time. As the day went on, it got very windy and the waves were much stronger. They were so high that Evan felt scared about going into the water.

- Anna's parents wanted to do something special for her birthday. They planned a party and didn't tell her. When the guests arrived, Anna felt surprised.

Directions

From two to five players can play this game. All you need is a die. Here are the rules:

1. The youngest player goes first.
2. He rolls the die and, using the key below, finds the feeling that matches the number rolled. If he rolls a six, he can choose the feeling.
3. He makes a face to show that feeling and tells about a time he experienced that feeling.
4. Going clockwise, the next player takes a turn.

happy   mad   sad   surprised   scared   your choice

Play this game a couple of times each week until you get very good at it. You can also make up other feelings to go with the numbers, like embarrassed, worried, frustrated, silly, and bored.

Expressing Your Feelings Creatively

Candace's teacher, Ms. Meyer, encouraged Candace to write in a journal whenever she felt upset. Ms. Meyer said that keeping a journal would help Candace learn about her feelings and start to feel better. Candace found it easier to type on the computer than to write by hand, and Ms. Meyer said that was okay. The important thing was to express her feelings about what had happened. Here is an example of one of her entries:

Today I had a terrible ride on the bus. The only seat free was next to a boy who took up most of the space. I could barely fit myself into the seat. I felt grouchy.

Her brother Sam liked to draw, and he found it easier to draw his feelings than to write about them. Sam used different colors and images to express how he felt.

Activity 20   Expressing Your Feelings Creatively

Directions

Expressing your feelings can help you cope with having TS. Here are some ways to do that. Read each idea and think about whether that would be a good tool for you.

Write "yes" if it would be a good tool for you.

Write "no" if it would not be a good tool for you.

Write "maybe" if it might be a good tool for you.

Writing in a journal   _____

Recording your thoughts   _____

Drawing   _____

Keeping a photo scrapbook   _____

Dictating to an adult   _____

Keeping a computer diary   _____

Other: _____   _____

Think about what your strongest feeling was today. In the space below, draw a picture that shows what happened to bring up that feeling.

Tyrone had different feelings about different rooms in his school. He liked when Ms. Smith helped him with reading, so he was usually happy to go to her room. He also liked recess and music. But when he went to the lunchroom, he sometimes felt embarrassed. His tics were noticeable, and not all the students who ate at the same time he did understood about his Tourette syndrome.

Tyrone usually liked going to the nurse's office. The nurse would give him a Band-Aid if he needed one and medicine when he needed it. The art room was a hard place for Tyrone. He was good at drawing cartoons because he had practiced those, but when the art teacher asked the class to try something new, Tyrone worried about it. If he didn't think he had done it well, he sometimes got mad. Then his teacher had him take a break from class, get a drink, and come back when he felt calm.

Directions

At school, you may have different feelings in different places. If you need help with these feelings, there are many people you can talk with. Some of these people are your teacher, the school nurse, the school counselor, and teachers' assistants.

Pretend that this is your school. Think about the way you usually feel in each place. Using this color key, outline the areas based on your feelings.

Orange = happy feelings
Red = mad feelings
Blue = sad feelings
Purple = worried feelings
Green = embarrassed feelings

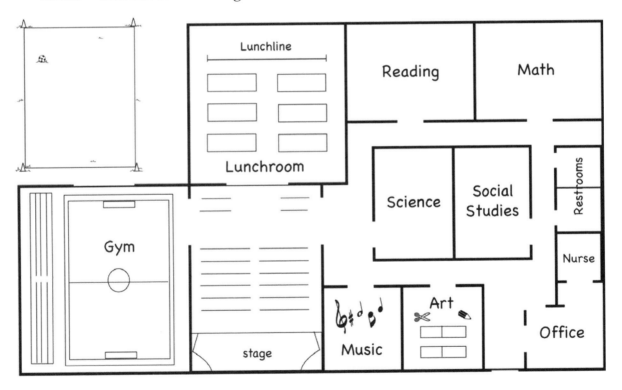

Tell where you often feel happy, and why. _____

_____

_____

Tell where you often feel worried, and why. _____

_____

_____

Which person at your school would you feel most comfortable talking with?

_____

_____

Getting Used to Middle School or Junior High

Ariel was going to start middle school in the fall. All summer, she worried about how she would manage. She knew she would have to change classrooms every fifty minutes. She would have only three minutes between classes to go to her locker if she needed anything and to get to her next class.

When she told her mother how she felt, her mother arranged for Ariel to visit the school before classes began. When they walked through the school, Ariel learned that odd-numbered rooms were on one side of the hall and even-numbered rooms were on the other side. There were two floors in her school, and rooms that started with a two-hundred number were on the second floor. The school secretary printed out Ariel's class schedule for her, and Ariel and her mom walked the route Ariel would have to take. They drew a map that Ariel could use to practice at home.

Ariel was also concerned that she would have a problem opening her lock, especially if she had to do it quickly. Her dad bought her a combination lock to practice on, and he wrote these instructions for her.

Hold the lock in the hand you do not write with.

Use your other hand to turn the dial to the right (clockwise). Clear the lock by turning the dial clockwise all the way around three times, without turning it back the other way (counterclockwise).

Then, keep turning clockwise and stop at the first number of your combination.

Now, turn the dial counterclockwise past the second number of your combination. Stop when you come to that number again.

Turn the dial clockwise and stop the first time you come to the third number of your combination.

Pull on the lock to open it.

They practiced together, and soon Ariel could open her lock easily.

When school started, she always kept a copy with her. After the first week of middle school, Ariel didn't even have to look at the classroom numbers anymore. She had to use her map only if there was a classroom change. Opening her lock was easy, and if she ever had a problem, she just looked at her instructions.

Directions

Look carefully at the map below and read all the room names.

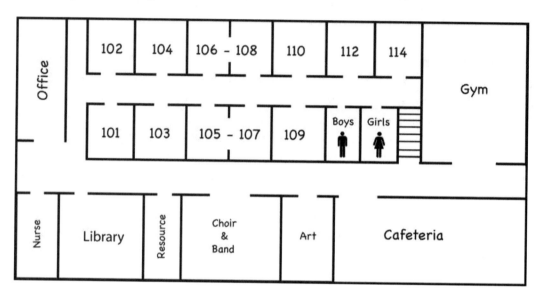

Follow these instructions:

Put an X on the band room, room 112, and room 103.
Draw a hamburger in the cafeteria.
Draw a pencil in the office.
Draw a line that goes down the hall from the gym to the library.
Draw a star on the restroom you would use.

Use your finger to trace Ariel's schedule:

Homeroom—room 102
Gym
English—room 110
Choir
Lunch
Math—room 105
Science—room 114
Social studies—room 101

Now plan a sample schedule that might be yours, and practice following it with your finger on the map.

Ross and his family went to religious services every week. When he was younger, he would go to children's services, where they sang songs and did art projects. It was okay for kids to be out of their seats. Now that he was older, Ross had to stay with his family, be quiet, and stand up and sit down only when everybody did. Having Tourette syndrome made that hard.

Ross and his parents wrote down the three rules that were most important for him to follow:

- Stand, sit, and kneel with everybody else.
- Be quiet during prayers.
- If you have to say something, whisper.

Ross also told his parents the three things he found hardest about going to services:

- Being quiet for a long time
- Getting dressed up with uncomfortable shoes
- People noticing his tics

After they looked at the lists, Ross and his parents worked out a plan. The first week, they came in just before services began. They sat near the back and left a little early, and Ross took two breaks. Each week, they changed the plan a little to help Ross slowly get used to staying the whole time. When Ross's TS was in its full-moon phase and particularly hard to manage, he would stay home with one of his parents and read Bible stories, sing songs, or plan a service project. These were other ways for him to show his faith.

Directions

Think about what going to religious services is like for you. List the three rules that are most important for you to follow:

1. _____

2. _____

3. _____

Put an X next to the rule that is the hardest for you.

Put a star next to the rule that is the easiest for you.

With a parent, read this list of ideas to see if any of them will make attending services easier for you. Put a check next to the ones that may help you.

_____ Wear clothing and shoes that are comfortable but appropriate.

_____ Ask someone to save you a seat, and come in just when the service is starting.

_____ Sit where your tics will be less noticeable, for example, in the last row.

_____ During a song or similar part of the service, take a break by getting a drink or going into the bathroom.

_____ Leave a little early.

_____ Volunteer to hand out bulletins or brochures before or after the service.

_____ Change seats.

_____ Go to a service that is less crowded or at a time of day that is easier for you.

_____ If services are video- or audiotaped, participate from home when your TS is intense, or in its full-moon phase.

_____ With your parent's permission, take a break from attending services, and use that time to do activities that relate to your religion.

_____ Talk privately with the person who leads the services to figure out a plan.

Write any other ideas here. _____

_____

_____

_____

_____

Now figure out a plan that will help you with a rule that is important for you to follow. Work on one problem at a time, and try different solutions until you find one that helps. Also remember that your Tourette syndrome changes, so your plan may need to change, too.

Use the space below to write about or draw what you are going to try.

Activity 24

Managing TS at the Movies

Christopher liked to go to the movies with his friend Syed. His parents tried to make sure that going to the movies would be a good experience for Christopher, as well as for the other people in the theater. When Christopher's tics were very intense, his parents suggested that he postpone going. He usually skipped opening weekends, when the crowds were likely to be large. Sometimes, Christopher and Syed went to matinees because fewer people were there, and Christopher's tics would not be so disturbing. Syed let Christopher choose their seats, and he picked ones where he would feel more at ease. The boys usually sat on an aisle, so that they could leave quickly when the movie was over, without bumping into other people.

With a little bit of planning, Christopher and Syed always had a good time at the movies—and so did everyone else.

Coping with Tourette Syndrome

Directions

Think about your last few trips to the movies. Look at the list below, and find some ideas that might make movie going more fun for you and maybe more pleasant for others. Put a check next to the ones you plan to try.

_____ Go to an early matinee.

_____ Sit on the aisle so you can take a break if you need to.

_____ Leave right after the movie to avoid the crowd.

_____ Ask someone to save you a seat so that you can come in right at the beginning of the movie.

_____ Sit closer to the front of the theater if you have vocal tics. Sound carries forward, so your tics will be less disturbing.

_____ Buy tickets in advance or at automated booths to avoid waiting in line.

_____ Chew something like a large piece of gum to help with vocal tics.

To help you decide which movies you would really like to see in a theater, use the rating scale below or create your own.

I have to see this movie right away, and I'll also buy the video when it is released
= * * * * *

I can wait a little while, but I'd like to see it within the first two weeks
= * * * *

I'll see it only if I'm having a good week with my TS
= * * *

I'll wait to rent it
= * *

I won't bother to see this movie
= *

Choose three movies that are playing now and rate them.

Movie: _____ Your rating: _____

Movie: _____ Your rating: _____

Movie: _____ Your rating: _____

Allison and her friend Chanel had a seventh-grade dance coming up. The girls and their moms went shopping at the mall to find dresses. Chanel looked for the most beautiful dress she could afford. Allison wanted to look good too, but she also had to think about what the dress would feel like. She couldn't stand scratchy fabrics or dresses that had lace or sequins around the neck. She liked fabrics that felt soft when she touched them. Blue was her favorite color, and Allison found a beautiful blue dress that was just right.

Jason's sister was getting married. He would be a junior usher and had to wear a tuxedo. His sister's fiancé wanted all the ushers to wear the same tuxedo, so Jason couldn't pick the one he wanted. When Jason and his dad went to get measured for their tuxedos, Jason had to stand very still while he was being measured, and that was hard for him to do. His dad ordered Jason's shirt one size larger than usual, because he knew that Jason couldn't stand anything tight around his neck.

Both Allison and Jason had to remember about Tourette syndrome and OCD in choosing clothing for special occasions.

Directions

The next time you have to shop for clothing for a special occasion, remember these helpful hints:

- Necklines can be a problem. Don't buy something that feels scratchy or tight.
- Watch out for tightness at the waist. Test it by sitting down. Does what you are trying on still look good and feel comfortable?
- Choose fabrics that feel comfortable to you.
- Sometimes new shoes hurt, so wear them a little each day before the special occasion.

Ask someone to take a picture of you dressed up. Tape a copy of it here.

How did you feel when you were dressed up? _____

_____

Tell about any problems you had with dressing up. _____

_____

What would you do the same next time? _____

_____

What would you do differently? _____

_____

Andrew didn't like to wait. He got fidgety and hyper when he had to wait in boring places. The places that were hardest were doctors' offices, restaurants, and long lines, no matter where. Andrew had always been restless even as a young child, and through the years, he and his mom had come up with many ideas to help him pass time.

When Andrew had a doctor's appointment, he always took a book or a pad of paper to draw on. When his family waited in long lines, they played games like "I Spy" and "The ABC Game." As Andrew got older, his parents made "The ABC Game" more challenging by picking harder topics. When Andrew and his family waited in a restaurant, they played "Silverware Tic-Tac-Toe" or card games. In the car, Andrew kept a backpack filled with time-passers. He didn't always need it, but it was very helpful when he did.

Directions

Where do you need to pass time? _____

_____

_____

What happens when you are bored? _____

_____

_____

What do you do to help pass time now? _____

_____

_____

Here are some suggestions for things to help you pass the time during car rides. Circle the ones you think would help you and then pack your own collection. Add other things that interest you—as long as they won't melt in the car!

Deck of cards	Magazines	Colored pencils and sharpener
Joke book	Small travel games	Origami book
Paper or notebook	Gum	Word searches
Small craft kits	Dice	Crossword-puzzle book
Pipe-cleaners	Books	Rubber-band ball
Comic books	Other: _____	

These activities need at least two people. Practice them so you will have more choices when you have to pass time.

Silverware Tic-Tac-Toe

Play tic-tac-toe with items on the restaurant table. Use forks and knives for the lines and sugar packets for the Xs and Os.

The ABC Game

Pick a topic like "animals," "boy's names," or "food." Take turns naming something in the topic, in ABC order. For example, if the topic is "animals," the first person could say "ant," the next person "bat," the third "cat," and so on until you get to Z. Players who can't think of something can pass. The person with the Z word gets to pick the next topic.

Name That Tune

One person hums a song or a commercial jingle, and the others try to name it. Whoever names it gets to hum the next tune.

Group Drawing

Use one piece of paper and pass it, in turn, to all players. The first person draws part of an object without telling anyone what it is. The next person adds to it, trying to make a picture. Keep passing the paper around until everyone in the group gets a chance to draw—or until dinner comes!

You can do these activities alone.

- Make people and animals from pipe cleaners.
- Interlock rubber bands with each other to form rubber-band chains.
- Drop a bouncy ball from different heights.
- Look through magazines to see how many different feelings you can name. This one is good for waiting in a doctor's office.

Nicole's family liked to go out to dinner on the weekends. In choosing a restaurant, Nicole and her parents always considered what phase her TS was in. When Nicole was having a difficult week, they would pick a place where they could be in and out quickly. When she was having a better week and her TS was in its crescent-moon phase, they would try someplace new or a restaurant where the wait might be longer.

No matter what restaurant Nicole's family picked, she always noticed where the restroom was in case she had to take a break from sitting at the table. She especially liked restaurants that had place mats for kids. She liked to draw and solve the puzzles to keep busy while waiting for her food. If her tics were particularly intense, Nicole sometimes took home her dessert to eat later. She would go to the car with her dad while her mom paid the bill.

Eating at the mall food court with her friends was usually easy for Nicole. The girls could each pick whatever type of food they wanted, which helped Nicole because she often had an obsession about having pizza. The food court was busy and noisy, so her tics were less noticeable, and if she saw other kids from school, she could usually get by with a wave or a short conversation.

Directions

Use the scale below to rate how easy or hard it is for you to cope with TS in these types of restaurants. If you also have ADHD or OCD, think about how it affects you in restaurants. Ask your parent to rate these as well.

Put a "1" next to restaurants that are easy for you.

Put a "2" next to restaurants that are okay for you, but not really easy.

Put a "3" next to restaurants that you find hard.

Put a star next to your favorite type of restaurant.

Type of Restaurant	Your Rating	Your Parent's Rating
Ice cream shop		
Sandwich shop		
Coffee place		
Fast food place		
Restaurant with four-course meals		
Restaurant with a patio		
Chinese restaurant		
Pizzeria		
Italian restaurant		
Buffet		
Pancake house		
Casual sit-down place		
Donut shop		
Restaurant with play area		

Compare your ratings with your parent's. Were they similar or different?

_____

_____

Here are some ideas that can help you in restaurants. Put a check next to the ones you think you will try.

_____ Choose a busy restaurant (or one that is often empty, if that is better for you).

_____ Sit in a booth. Sounds carry less and motions are less noticeable.

_____ Take a break by going to the restroom or, with a grown-up, by sitting in the car for a short time.

_____ Distract yourself with activities on the place mat.

_____ Look at the menu online, so you can order as soon as you sit down.

_____ Call ahead to put your name on the waiting list.

_____ Use a time-passer from Activity 26.

_____ Find the best place to sit for you. It might be in a tucked-away booth or near the restroom or near a window.

_____ If you know you will be very hungry, bring a snack or ask for crackers.

Try some of these ideas the next time you eat out. Tell how they worked.

_____

_____

_____

_____

Hilary really liked to shop, especially at the mall in her town. She planned to go there at times when her TS was less intense, and she never went around holidays when it would be really crowded. There were some stores that Hilary liked no matter when she went, like the video store. She liked to read all the DVD cases and pick out one to take home. The aisles were wide enough that she didn't worry about bumping into someone if she had to kick, which was one of her motor tics. Buying food for her fish at the pet shop was hard for her; she always wanted to buy another pet when she was there. Her OCD made it very hard for Hilary to follow her mom's rules in the pet shop, and she often felt embarrassed there.

Directions

Use the scale below to rate how easy or hard it is for you to cope with TS when shopping in these places. If you also have ADHD or OCD, think about how it affects you in stores. Ask your parent to rate these as well.

Put a "1" next to places that are easy for you.

Put a "2" next to places that are okay for you, but not really easy.

Put a "3" next to places that you find hard.

Put a star next to your favorite place to shop.

Place to Shop	Your Rating	Your Parent's Rating
Video store		
Small grocery store		
Supermarket		
Drugstore		
Mall		
Festival or bazaar		
Dollar store		
Gift shop		
Candy store		
Pet shop		

Did your parent agree with your ratings? _____

Review the following ideas with your parent and then pick a few to try when you are planning a shopping trip. Put a check next to the ones that look like good ideas for you.

_____ If your TS is intense, consider only shopping in places you rated 1 or 2.

_____ If you are in a less intense phase, try ones you rated 3.

_____ Before going to a store, look at websites to help you decide what you want.

_____ Before you go to a mall, look online for a map of its layout. Use it to plan what stores you will go to.

_____ Shop for short periods, taking breaks when you need them.

_____ Try going to a difficult shopping place first and then an easier place.

_____ Distract yourself with your favorite music and earphones.

_____ Shop for someone else instead of yourself. Leave as soon as you have found something.

Contagion: New Tics and Behaviors

When Blake and his father went to the supermarket, Blake carried the shopping list, and his dad pushed the cart. Blake also helped with the coupons and with choosing the cereal and frozen pizza. They really tried to follow their list and not buy extra things, but it didn't always work. By the time they got to the checkout line, they might have an ice cream treat that Blake picked up and hot peppers that nobody but his dad would eat. Sometimes, they were surprised to see what was in their cart!

The same thing can happen with TS or OCD. Sometimes, people accidentally pick up new tics or compulsive behaviors from other people or from movies, without even realizing it at first. It is called "contagion." It is kind of like watching someone else yawn and then feeling like you have to yawn, too. Tics and behaviors that come from contagion usually only last for a short time, and using humor can be a good way to manage them. Look back at Activity 13 to help you remember how to use humor.

Directions

Circle your answers to the questions below:

Have you ever seen someone's behavior and then done the same thing?	Yes	No	Maybe
Have you ever heard a noise and then made the same noise?	Yes	No	Maybe
Have you ever watched a movie and copied something from it?	Yes	No	Maybe
Do you think you have ever had contagion?	Yes	No	Maybe
If so, has contagion ever happened in school?	Yes	No	Maybe
Has it ever happened at home?	Yes	No	Maybe

Tell about what happened. _____

_____

_____

_____

_____

Garrett thought his grandma was great. She always asked him what he had been doing at school and often sent him little cards just so he would know she was thinking about him. Every year, his family went to Grandma's house for Thanksgiving, and Garrett always looked forward to going. Holidays at Grandma's were fun, but sometimes Garrett got in trouble for not following the rules of the house. These were Grandma's rules:

- Eat only in the kitchen.
- Play in the living room, the den, or the guestroom, but not the kitchen.
- Come to the table when you are called.
- Ask to be excused before leaving the table.
- When you are outdoors, stay in the backyard.
- Don't go into Grandma's room without permission.

They weren't hard rules to follow, but they were different from the rules at Garrett's house and sometimes he forgot. His parents always reminded Garrett that it was important to remember the rules at other people's houses, and they helped him try to remember Grandma's rules.

Directions

Think of a house you visit often. Whose is it? _____

_____

What is fun about being at this house? _____

_____

_____

What makes it hard to be in this house? _____

_____

_____

Tell some of the rules at this house. _____

_____

_____

_____

Tell any special rules for playing outside this house. _____

_____

_____

_____

Pretend the house below is one you visit frequently.

Label each room.

If you are not allowed to go into a room without permission, color it red.
If you are allowed to go into a room but not to play there, color it yellow.
If you are allowed to play in a room, color it green.

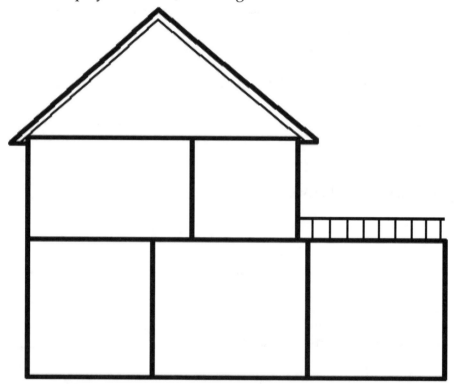

Put a star on your favorite room. Tell why it is your favorite. _____

_____

Circle any room where you might have a hard time following the rules.

Who could help you follow the rules in this house? _____

_____

Hosting Parties

Whitney's birthday was coming up. Her mom knew that it was important for the birthday party to be well planned so that Whitney could enjoy it. Whitney, her sister Megan, and their mom started planning three weeks before the big day.

Whitney wanted to have a swimming party at the local pool. Her mom said that was fine, but they should have another idea ready in case it rained. Megan suggested renting movies; the girls could sit on their towels and have an indoor picnic. Whitney had wanted to serve pizza, but one of her friends was allergic to cheese, so she decided to have tacos instead. Everyone could make their own tacos just the way they wanted them.

Directions

Planning ahead can make hosting a party easier—and more fun! Talk with your parent about your party, and read the ideas on the left to help you get ready. Use the space on the right to make notes about what you will do.

Date and time of your party _____ Place _____

Invitations

Party Planning Ideas	What You Will Do
Ask your parent how many kids you may invite.	
An even number of guests often makes a party run more smoothly.	
Mail your invitations at least two weeks in advance.	
If you are giving out invitations in person, be careful not to hurt anyone's feelings by doing it in front of kids who aren't invited.	
Consider including the names of everyone invited so friends know whom to talk to about the party.	

Activities

Party Planning Ideas	What You Will Do
Plan the schedule with your parent.	
If the party is at your house, plan at least three different activities to do. Don't be upset if you don't get to all three.	
Rent one or two movies for a back-up plan. Watch them ahead of time to be sure you've chosen good ones.	
Ask someone to take pictures during the party, and make copies for your friends.	
Let your parent be in charge of any medications.	

Food and Drinks

Party Planning Ideas	What You Will Do
Pick foods that most kids enjoy, perhaps pizza or hot dogs.	
If any of your friends have allergies, be sure to have food available that they can eat.	
Make cleaning up easier by avoiding drinks that are purple or red.	
Pick drinks that do not have caffeine.	
Use disposable plates and cups.	

After your party is over, answer the following questions.

Did you have a good time? Tell why or why not. _____

_____

Do you think your guests had a good time? Tell why or why not. _____

_____

Do your parents think the party went well? Tell why or why not. _____

_____

Is there anything you would do differently for your next party? _____

_____

In the space below, paste a photograph or draw a picture of your party.

_____

Going to Sleepovers

Cameron and his friends loved to play video games. One weekend during summer vacation, his friends decided to have a video-game sleepover. They planned to order pizza and play video games all evening. Cameron thought that the video-game part was a great idea, but he wasn't so sure about the sleepover. He had been to two sleepover parties before, but he hadn't been able to stay overnight. Both times, he had gotten nervous and felt sick, and he had had to leave. Cameron was embarrassed that his friends thought he was too scared to stay the night.

His mom understood that having Tourette syndrome made sleeping away from home hard for Cameron. She suggested that if Cameron didn't feel ready to stay overnight he could make an excuse, like having an early doctor's appointment the next morning. His mom said that lots of kids leave sleepovers without staying overnight.

But Cameron really wanted to go to the video-game party and to stay the night, so he and his mom thought about ways to make it easier for him. Here are the ideas they came up with:

- Practice sleeping on the floor in your sleeping bag.
- Take your own pillow with you.
- Wear a T-shirt and shorts if you feel self-conscious about being in pajamas.
- Stay over at a relative's house first for practice.
- Bring your own music to listen to; remember to bring headphones.

After talking with his mom, Cameron felt better. He was able to go to the party and sleep over. When it was time to go to sleep and he started to feel upset, he put on his headphones and listened to music until he relaxed. At breakfast the next morning, all the boys agreed that they had had a great time.

Directions

List ideas that can help you stay at a sleepover. You can use Cameron's suggestions or come up with your own.

_____

_____

_____

The next time you go to a sleepover, answer these questions:

What did you do to prepare for the sleepover? _____

_____

_____

Before you went, did you expect to come home or stay all night?

_____

_____

Did it work out the way you expected? _____

_____

_____

In this box, draw a picture that shows how you felt when it was time to go to the sleepover.

Now, draw a picture that shows how you felt when you came home.

Remember, just because you haven't been successful at sleeping over before doesn't mean that it won't work next time. Keep trying!

Keeping Score When You Shouldn't

Keeping score was part of Carlos's OCD. He kept score of how many home runs his baseball team had and how many foul shots his favorite basketball player made. That kind of scorekeeping was okay; it was part of the game. But Carlos also kept score of other things, like how often his brother sat in the front seat of the car or chose the TV show they would watch. Keeping score like that just made his brother mad. At school, he counted how many times each kid had been first in line and how often the teacher called his name. If he thought someone had been unfair, he got very angry. The kids at school didn't like when Carlos kept score that way. His teacher explained that other kids didn't usually count those kinds of things.

Carlos wanted to stop keeping score at times when he shouldn't. His parents understood that his OCD made it hard for him to do that, and they promised to help. With Carlos and his counselor, they decided on the following ideas for Carlos to try:

1. Remind yourself not to keep score ahead of time.
2. Avoid these situations if you need to in order to keep your cool.
3. Pick someone to try to help instead, and help that person.
4. Tell a friend that you sometimes need to keep score.
5. Ask a friend to help you pick something different to do.
6. Make a deal to take turns on a schedule. For example, you get to choose your seat in the car on even days and your brother gets to choose on odd days.

Directions

List three games you have played for which you should keep score:

1. _____

2. _____

3. _____

List three games you have played for which you shouldn't keep score:

1. _____

2. _____

3. _____

Tell about times when you keep score, even though you shouldn't.

_____

_____

_____

Pick two of Carlos's ideas that you think will help you. Write them here.

_____

_____

After you have tried them, tell what happened.

_____

_____

_____

Activity 34   Being a Good Loser and a
                              Good Winner

James loved to play games. He played video games, board games, and team sports.
When James won, he was very happy. He would jump up and down and brag a lot.
When he lost, James got mad. He would throw things and act grumpy. When he
played with his brother, his parents encouraged him to act better, whether he won or
lost. His coach made him sit out if he got mad and threw things.

Whether James was playing with his brother or his friends or on a team, other kids
didn't like how he acted. His counselor suggested that they work on ways for James
to be a better loser—and a better winner. She told him that it was okay to be happy
when he won, but that other kids would be more likely to play with him again if he
didn't brag so much. She also helped James learn to keep his temper when he lost.
They played games in which they could each win and lose so that James could practice
staying calm.

Sometimes James and his counselor took turns role-playing other people, like his
brother, the coach, or his teammates. This helped James understand the feelings of
those people when he played for real.

Directions

In the space below, draw a picture of you playing the game you most like to win.

How do you act when you win this game? _____

_____

How do you act when you lose this game? _____

_____

List three other games you have played in which there are winners and losers.

1. _____

2. _____

3. _____

Do you need to practice being a good winner? _____

Do you need to practice being a good loser? _____

Tell what you will do to be better at winning and at losing. _____

_____

_____

_____

With another person, play a game in which winning is not important to you. You might choose a game that you don't play any longer or one that you have outgrown. Try to lose without the other player knowing.

Tell how you felt playing this game. _____

_____

Now try to lose at a game that you love to win.

Tell how you felt playing this game. _____

_____

Organizing for Morning and Evening

Jaye was wide-awake in the morning. She got up easily and was usually ready for school early. She was never late and felt most energetic in the morning. Jaye liked having the classes she found most difficult in the morning.

Michael's mother called him a "night owl" because he liked to stay up late. He had trouble getting up in the morning and tried very hard not to be late for school. He had the most energy in the afternoon and had trouble getting to sleep at night.

Directions

Getting ready for the day can be easier if you know whether you are a morning person or a night person. Think about which you are, and draw a picture of the sun or the moon to show which describes you better. If you can't decide, ask your parent to help you.

If you are you a morning person, try these suggestions:

- Finish your homework soon after school.
- Review for tests before you feel sleepy.
- Go to bed at the same time each night and plan to get up early.
- Make your lunch in the morning.

Write any other ideas here. _____

_____

If you are a night person, try these suggestions:

- Try different alarm clocks or music until you find the one that wakes you best.
- Put what you need for school near the door you will leave by.
- Choose your clothes for the next day before you go to sleep.
- After dinner, make your lunch for the next day.

Write any other ideas here. _____

_____

Organizing for Morning and Evening

In the space that follows, plan a routine that will help you be organized. Keep it simple and schedule the most for the time of day you are most energetic. You can make copies of this routine and post them where they will help you most: your bedroom door, the refrigerator, the bathroom mirror, and so on.

My Morning Routine	My Evening Routine

Jasmine had a problem getting to sleep. During the school week, she was often awake for a long time after going to bed. She was always tired in the morning, and sometimes she was late to school. After Jasmine had been late several times, her teacher spoke with her. He explained that kids, and especially kids with TS, need resting time; their brains need a chance to pause. He gave Jasmine a special assignment—to write a list of ideas that could help her improve her sleep routine.

Jasmine learned that kids in elementary school need about ten hours of sleep each night, and kids in middle school need about nine hours. She listed these ideas:

- I will have a bedtime routine to help me go to sleep more easily.
- I will follow my routine even on weekends.
- I will turn off the TV or stop playing video games at least thirty minutes before bedtime.
- I won't have cola or anything else with caffeine in the evening.
- I will make sure I am warm enough in bed, especially my feet.

After Jasmine had tried these ideas for a while, she found getting to sleep was much easier.

Directions

Think about your sleep routine, and answer the questions below.

On school nights, how many hours of sleep do you actually get? _____

Do you stay up really late on weekends?   Yes   No

Are you especially tired on Monday mornings? If you are, tell why you think that is so.

_____

_____

_____

If you wake up during the night, tell why. _____

_____

_____

If you get out of bed during the night, tell why. _____

_____

_____

Use the space below to plan a new bedtime routine for weeknights.

1. In the pillow, write three calming thoughts (for example: clouds floating by).
2. At the top of the blanket, write what time you will start getting ready for bed.
3. In the middle of the blanket, write the routine you will follow.
4. At the bottom of the blanket, write what time you want to be asleep by.

Make copies of your routine, and post them where you will see them in the evenings: on your bedroom door, on the bathroom mirror, and on your bedside table.

Studying for Tests

When Dylan had a test coming up, he had to spend extra time studying. Reading was hard for him, so he drew pictures to help him remember information. He would write words on the front of index cards and draw pictures that illustrated the words on the back. Here are some cards Dylan made when his science class studied life cycles.

Katie had a different way to study for tests. She made up word tricks to help her memorize facts. Her class learned the order of the planets from closest to the sun to farthest away: **M**ercury, **V**enus, **E**arth, **M**ars, **J**upiter, **S**aturn, **U**ranus, **N**eptune, **P**luto. To help her remember the order, she used this sentence:

My **V**ery **E**ducated **M**other **J**ust **S**erved **U**s **N**ine **P**ies.

Directions

Read the list of study tips below. Put a star next to ones you've tried and found helpful. Put an X next to any you've tried that didn't help you. Put a check next to tips you plan to try.

_____ Set up a study area in a quiet spot that you can use every day, away from the television or video games.

_____ Make sure your seat is comfortable.

_____ Keep a shelf or box with study items nearby.

_____ Study with music if it helps you block out other distractions. Some people study better with total quiet.

_____ Decide in advance whether you will want a snack. If you will, get it before you start studying.

_____ Take a break when you need to.

_____ Study with a friend.

Studying for Tests

Here is a word trick to help you remember some good study habits:

Take time to organize, and study for two or three days.

Eat a good breakfast.

Study what your teacher tells you to.

Try reviewing right before bed.

Set up a quick review the morning of the test.

Now make up one of your own:

Start by _____

Try to _____

Understand _____

Don't _____

You can _____

List five states in the United States and make up a word trick to help you remember them.

1. _____

2. _____

3. _____

4. _____

5. _____

Activity 38   Taking Tests

Lindsey used to get very nervous before and during tests. When her teacher announced that she would be giving an afterschool lesson on test-taking skills, Lindsey decided to go. She hoped it would help her improve her test grades in the subjects that were hardest for her. The teacher explained how important it was to review before the test, to relax during the test, and to remain focused. At the end of the class, she handed out the following summary of what she had taught.

Taking Tests

The night before or the morning of the test

1. Review your study materials.
2. Check to see if you have everything you need, like pencils, pens, or a calculator.

Before starting the test

1. Put your feet flat on the floor and your hands on your lap or desk.
2. Slowly breathe in and out twice
3. Look down at the test or your desk.
4. Think back to your studying.
5. Breathe in and out slowly again.
6. Listen to your teacher's directions.

During the test

1. Write your name and the date and any other information your teacher has asked for.
2. Look through the test briefly.
3. Answer all the questions you know and skip others.
4. Read directions for each new section of the test.
5. Go back over the test and try to answer the questions you skipped.

Directions

The next time you have a test coming up, review the test-taking strategies on the previous page. After the test, answer these questions:

Did you have all the supplies you needed for the test with you?	Yes	No
Did you follow directions?	Yes	No
Do you think your studying helped you get a better grade?	Yes	No
Did the questions look like the information you studied?	Yes	No
Did you change any answers?	Yes	No
Did you finish on time?	Yes	No

What would you do the same for your next test? _____

_____

_____

_____

What would you do differently? _____

_____

_____

_____

Matthew's older sister, Emily, tried hard to understand about Tourette syndrome. She read about it on the Internet, and she asked Matthew lots of questions. When he had a hard time with his schoolwork, Emily helped him study. She was always patient about his tics. His older brother, Corey, thought that Matthew was a bother. He didn't understand why their family had to go to certain restaurants or change vacation plans because of Matthew's Tourette syndrome.

Matthew's parents decided to have a family meeting and give everyone a chance to talk about it. Corey was pleased because he would be able to talk about how he was affected by Matthew's having TS. Matthew was pleased because he would be able help Corey understand by sharing what he knew about TS. Having a family meeting would give everyone a chance to share, learn, and make changes.

Directions

Name your brother(s) here: _____

_____

Name your sister(s) here: _____

_____

What activities from this book would you like to share with them? _____

_____

Write or draw the most important thing that you want them to know.

Now ask them these questions and write their answers here.

What is the most important thing you want me to know? _____

_____

_____

_____

What questions do you have for me? _____

_____

_____

_____

Write your answer to their questions here. _____

_____

_____

_____

Revisiting the Phases of TS

Activity 3 compared Tourette syndrome to the phases of the moon. Here is a review:

- **When my TS is like a crescent moon,** I have fewer tics and I feel happy most of the time.

- **When my TS is like a half moon,** I feel frustrated. It is hard for me to finish my schoolwork and my chores at home.

- **When my TS is like a three-quarter moon,** it is hard for me to handle. I worry more, and I need more help from my parents and teachers.

- **When my TS is like a full moon,** I feel like saying, "Forget it!" I get angry, so I talk with my counselor more often. I need help from grown-ups to explain to other kids what is happening.

Directions

Think about what TS is like for you in each phase, and answer the questions that follow.

Crescent

What are your tics like? _____

What do you find easy to do? _____

What do you find hard to do? _____

What is school like? _____

What kind of restaurants and stores are easiest for you during this phase? _____

_____

What kind of help do you need during this phase? _____

_____

What is important for you to remember during this phase? _____

_____

Half

What are your tics like? _____

What do you find easy to do? _____

What do you find hard to do? _____

What is school like? _____

What kind of restaurants and stores are easiest for you during this phase? _____

_____

What kind of help do you need during this phase? _____

_____

What is important for you to remember during this phase? _____

_____

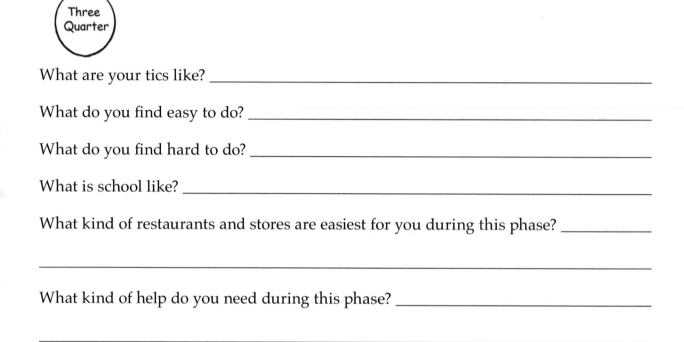

Three Quarter

What are your tics like? _____

What do you find easy to do? _____

What do you find hard to do? _____

What is school like? _____

What kind of restaurants and stores are easiest for you during this phase? _____

_____

What kind of help do you need during this phase? _____

_____

What is important for you to remember during this phase? _____

_____

(Full)

What are your tics like? _____

What do you find easy to do? _____

What do you find hard to do? _____

What is school like? _____

What kind of restaurants and stores are easiest for you during this phase? _____

_____

What kind of help do you need during this phase? _____

_____

What is important for you to remember during this phase? _____

_____

Parent Appendix: About Coprolalia

While coprolalia is a well-known tic, it is not common; of every hundred people who have TS, only about ten have coprolalia. If your child seems to have a problem with coprolalia, talk to a health professional to make sure that the problem is actually coprolalia. You will need to determine how often it occurs and what seems to make it worse and to work with your child's school to address it in a way that considers your child's needs and the needs of others at school.

If coprolalia is a rare occurrence, you can arrange for your child to visit the principal's office after an incident of cursing, as any other child would. A knowledgeable adult can interview the child to determine whether the cursing was a manifestation of TS. Trust and truth on both sides are very important. A formal written plan should be implemented if this occurs more than once or twice.

If coprolalia is a common problem for your child, there may need to be intervention in the classroom, and other students can be taught to ignore the behavior. The teacher is the best role model for student responses. A class talk would be appropriate, with all the adults present working as a team during the talk. Your plan also needs to address how to inform substitute teachers and other school personnel.

No matter what the approach to handling coprolalia, your child and all involved adults need to work as a team; as the parent you will often be required to take the lead. You may be called upon to explain it to new people and in public. Your child should be encouraged to say "Excuse me" or "I'm sorry," as that is what would be expected in the outside community.

It is also important that the presence of coprolalia be documented in counseling and medical records, in the event of future legal issues.

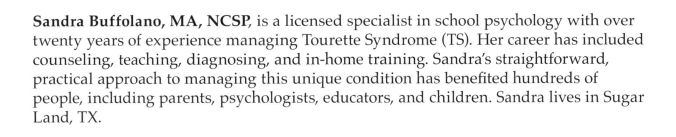

Sandra Buffolano, MA, NCSP, is a licensed specialist in school psychology with over twenty years of experience managing Tourette Syndrome (TS). Her career has included counseling, teaching, diagnosing, and in-home training. Sandra's straightforward, practical approach to managing this unique condition has benefited hundreds of people, including parents, psychologists, educators, and children. Sandra lives in Sugar Land, TX.

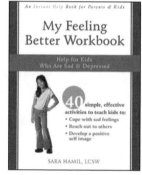